GETTING TO KNOW THE WORLD'S GREATEST
INVENTORS & SCIENTISTS

THOMAS
EDISON

Inventor with a Lot of Bright Ideas

WRITTEN AND ILLUSTRATED BY MIKE VENEZIA

CHILDREN'S PRESS®
AN IMPRINT OF SCHOLASTIC INC.
NEW YORK   TORONTO   LONDON   AUCKLAND   SYDNEY
MEXICO CITY   NEW DELHI   HONG KONG
DANBURY, CONNECTICUT

Reading Consultant: Nanci R. Vargus, EdD, Assistant Professor, School of Education, University of Indianapolis

Content Consultant: Joyce Bedi, Senior Historian, Lemelson Center for the Study of Invention and Innovation, National Museum of American History, Smithsonian Institution

Photographs © 2009: age fotostock/Dennis MacDonald: 22; Corbis Images: 29 (Bettmann), 23 (Mathew B. Brady), 31 bottom (Hulton-Deutsch Collection); Library of Congress/Metropolitan Print Company: 30; Nick Romanenko: 20; North Wind Picture Archives: 26, 27; Photo Researchers, NY/SPL: 18; The Art Archive/Picture Desk: 3 (Culver Pictures), 28 bottom (National Archives, Washington DC); The Granger Collection, New York: 8, 13, 31 top; The Image Works: 14, 15 (Mary Evans Picture Library), 24 (SSPL), 21 (Topham); U.S. Department of the Interior, National Park Service, Edison National Historic Site: 28 top.

Colorist for illustrations: Andrew Day

Library of Congress Cataloging-in-Publication Data

Venezia, Mike.
  Thomas Edison : inventor with a lot of bright ideas / written and illustrated by Mike Venezia.
      p. cm. — (Getting to know the world's greatest inventors and scientists)
  Includes index.
  ISBN-13: 978-0-531-14978-2 (lib. bdg.)   978-0-531-22209-6 (pbk.)
  ISBN-10: 0-531-14978-1 (lib. bdg.)   0-531-22209-8 (pbk.)
  1. Edison, Thomas A. (Thomas Alva), 1847-1931—Juvenile literature. 2. Inventors—United States—Biography—Juvenile literature. 3. Electric engineers—United States—Biography—Juvenile literature. I. Title. II. Series.

  TK140.E3V46 2009
  621.3092—dc22
  [B]
                          2008002306

11 12 13 14 15 R 20 19 18 17   62

Scholastic Inc., 557 Broadway, New York, NY 10012.

Thomas Edison in his laboratory in 1915

Thomas Alva Edison was born on February 11, 1847, in Milan, Ohio. Edison was one of the all-time greatest inventors. During his life, he came up with more than 1,000 inventions that helped move the world into the modern age.

Some of Edison's inventions were so amazing that people started calling him the Wizard of Menlo Park. Menlo Park is the New Jersey town where Thomas Edison set up his first large **laboratory.** He called it his "invention factory," and he came up with his most famous inventions there. Thomas hired the best scientists, electrical engineers, and thinkers to help him invent the **phonograph,** the first successful light bulb, and the first movie camera.

Thomas Edison loved hard work. He expected his team to put in long hours every day. Thomas knew how to keep his employees happy, though. For fun, they went fishing and had barbeques. They'd make up wacky songs around a pipe organ Thomas installed in the lab.

Before Thomas Edison's light bulb came along, people had to light their homes with candles or smelly, dangerous gas lamps. A lot of people think Edison invented the light bulb. Actually, he didn't invent the light bulb, he perfected it. Other inventors had been able to make electric light bulbs, but these weren't very bright and they didn't last very long. Thomas Edison was the first person to make a usable, long-lasting light bulb.

Maybe even more important than perfecting the light bulb was the way Edison figured out how to supply electricity to homes, businesses, and schools across the country. It was a huge job. Edison's hard work helped make it possible for millions of people in the world today to just flip a switch and get electrical light and power whenever they want.

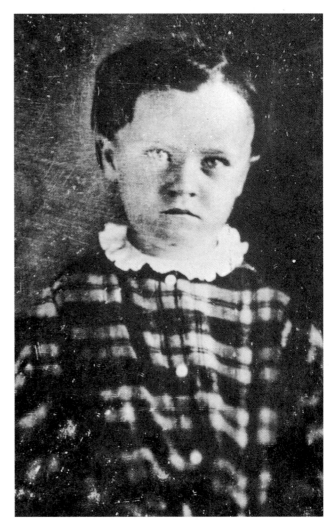

Thomas Alva Edison at the age of three

When Thomas Edison was about seven, his family moved from Milan, Ohio, to Port Huron, Michigan. Thomas started school in Port Huron. He didn't do very well, though. Thomas daydreamed a lot. Plus, he couldn't hear very well. Thomas had some serious ear infections that left him partially deaf. Thomas Edison's teacher thought he was just a confused, mixed-up, hopeless student.

Mrs. Edison ended up taking her son out of school. Thomas got a good education at home. His mother knew her son was smart, and had no problem teaching him. Thomas began reading every book he could find. He loved books about science, especially those that explained how electricity worked.

While growing up, Thomas Edison wanted to
learn as much as he possibly could. He set up
experimental laboratories any place he could. He
sometimes got in trouble when his experiments
got out of hand. Once, Thomas accidentally
burned down his father's barn! Another time,
he filled the house with smoke while doing an
experiment in the basement.

When Thomas Edison was 13 years old, he
got a job on the Grand Trunk Railroad. Thomas

sold newspapers, candy, and fruit to passengers. A friendly conductor let Thomas set up a laboratory in the baggage car. Thomas did experiments in his spare time. He also set up his own newspaper business in the baggage car. He bought a printing press, wrote news stories, and printed the paper. He called it the *Weekly Herald*. Thomas's paper didn't last very long, though. One day, while Thomas was experimenting in his laboratory, the baggage car caught fire.

After the fire, Thomas wasn't allowed to experiment in the baggage car any more. Next, Thomas decided to learn about the **telegraph.** All train stations had telegraph offices to deliver news about train schedules. The telegraph was the latest and coolest technology at the time. The telegraph system allowed people to send coded messages over a wire to people miles away.

This photograph shows Edison at the age of thirteen, when he sold fruit, candy, and newspapers on the Grand Trunk Railway.

When Thomas was younger, he had played around with telegraphy. He built his own telegraph line between his house and a friend's house.

Thomas decided he wanted to become a telegraph operator. He asked a stationmaster to help him improve his skills at reading and sending messages in **Morse code**.

This was the beginning of an exciting adventure for young Tom Edison. At the age of sixteen, Thomas began working as a telegraph operator. He traveled from state to state, working at various telegraph offices.

In the 1860s, when Edison was a teenager, the telegraph was the fastest form of long-distance communication. Telegraph lines stretched across the nation (above).

Like the men in this photograph, young Thomas Edison worked as a telegraph operator.

As an operator, Thomas was always figuring out ways to improve the telegraph systems he was using. Even as a teenager, Thomas amazed his bosses by finding ways to send messages farther, with fewer mistakes. Most of Thomas's bosses allowed him to set up an area where he could work on experiments when he wasn't busy sending and receiving messages.

Thomas Edison always had a good sense of humor. At least *he* thought he had a good sense of humor. One of Thomas's favorite practical jokes at his job was to hook up an electrical wire to the office water tank. He got a big kick out of watching workers get jolted when they went to get a drink.

In 1868, Thomas moved to Boston, Massachusetts, to work at the largest telegraph company in the world, Western Union. He continued experimenting in his spare time. Thomas came up with a way to send more than one message over a telegraph wire at the same time. Before this advancement, a single wire could be tied up for hours. Now people wouldn't have to wait so long to deliver or receive messages.

Thomas's improvement was a big deal. It gave Thomas the confidence to leave his job and become a full-time inventor.

This automatic vote recorder was Edison's first patented invention. It was meant to speed up the voting process in Congress. But Congress ended up rejecting the machine. Politicians often wanted to slow the process down so that they'd have time to convince other politicians to change their votes!

Thomas Edison's first **patented** invention was an electric vote recorder. Inventors patent their ideas so no one else can take credit for them. The inventor submits his or her plans to a government patent office. If the invention is original, it is awarded its own special patent number. The patent prevents other people from making or selling the invention.

Even though Thomas's vote recorder worked perfectly, it was a big flop. No one was interested in it. Amazingly, Thomas Edison didn't let it bother him one bit. He considered his failure to be a good lesson. He promised himself he would never invent anything unless people really wanted it.

Thomas Edison's attitude about failing was one of the reasons he became so successful. He wasn't afraid to take chances. If something didn't work, he would find out why, and then not repeat that mistake.

In 1869, Thomas moved from Boston to New York City. He continued to work on ways to improve the telegraph. He came up with other interesting ideas, too. Soon Thomas's inventions began to earn him lots of money.

An improved stock ticker was one of Edison's first major inventions. A ticker is an electronic device that receives telegraph messages and prints them out on a strip of paper. A **stock** ticker could quickly print price information for people who were buying and selling stocks.

Thomas used the money to set up his own small laboratory. He hired assistants and got right to work inventing more things.

As busy as he was, Thomas found time to date a girl he had met in one of the telegraph offices where he had worked. Her name was Mary Stilwell. In 1871, Thomas and Mary got married. Over the next few years, they had three children.

When Thomas Edison was 24 years old, he married Mary Stilwell (right). Together they had three children: Marion, Thomas Jr., and William.

In 1875, Thomas Edison made plans to move his laboratory to a new location. He chose Menlo Park, a small, quiet town in New Jersey. Thomas had a large, two-story lab built there, as well as a machine shop, library, and office. Thomas hired more people. They worked hard, thinking up hundreds of amazing inventions.

A team of talented workers helped Edison at his Menlo Park laboratory. Today, people can visit a replica of the laboratory at Historic Greenfield Village in Dearborn, Michigan (above).

Edison's phonograph was the world's first sound-recording machine. Here he is shown with an early model of the phonograph.

One amazing invention was the phonograph. This was the first machine that could record and play back someone's voice. At first, the sound wasn't that good. Thomas knew he could fix it but decided to put the phonograph aside for a while. That gave him time to concentrate on a bigger idea, the **incandescent** light bulb.

Incandescent bulbs contain a thin string or wire called a **filament**. The bulb glows when an **electric current** passes through the filament and heats it up. Thomas began searching for just the right material to make a filament that would last for a long time.

Thomas and his team spent over a year testing thousands of filament materials. All of them seemed to burn up or break as soon as an electrical current was connected to the bulb. Finally, Thomas and his assistants made an important discovery. When they baked a cotton thread, it turned into **carbon.** This filament burned for hours! They also discovered that if all the air was sucked out of the bulb, which created a **vacuum,** the filament lasted even longer. Edison had invented a light bulb that really worked.

This is a replica of the first successful incandescent light bulb. Thomas Edison invented it in 1879.

Thomas Edison worked harder than ever during this period. He was happy with the work he was doing on the light bulb, but his wife and their children were not. Thomas was so busy he often slept at the lab, and sometimes didn't come home for weeks at a time. His family hardly got to see him.

Thomas demonstrated his light bulb to news reporters and crowds of curious people. Then he devised a plan to supply enough electricity to light up towns and cities. This was a huge job. Thomas had to raise money from **investors** for the project. He had to convince government officials to let him dig up streets in New York City and install electrical cables underground. He'd also need to build a power station that could provide enough electricity to light up many buildings.

In 1882, workers in New York City prepared the way for electricity by laying electrical cables underneath the city's streets.

Electric lights at Times Square in New York in the early 1900s

Thomas got the permission he needed. On September 4, 1882, after a year of construction, he flipped the switch at the first electrical power station. More than 800 light bulbs in 25 buildings began to glow! Thomas Edison suddenly became one of the most famous and wealthy men in the world.

Sadly, things didn't go well for long. In the middle of Thomas's great successes, his wife, Mary, died. Thomas Edison was terribly saddened.

Edison with his second wife, Mina (seated), and their three children (from left to right): Madeleine, Theodore, and Charles

Thomas eventually remarried and started a second family. This time, he made a point to spend more time with his wife and children.

In 1887, Thomas built a new and much larger laboratory in West Orange, New Jersey. He got back to perfecting his favorite invention, the phonograph.

An advertisement for an Edison phonograph

Thomas Edison went on to find new ways to mine iron. He started a cement company, and improved the **rechargeable storage battery**. In the early 1900s, Edison supplied batteries to **manufacturers** of **electric cars**. Battery-powered automobiles didn't catch on at the time. Today, they are finally starting to get attention.

Edison and his son in an electric car

Thomas Alva Edison was also responsible for starting the most popular entertainment industry of all time, the movie business! Thomas invented the movie camera and helped develop the movie projector. He built the first movie studio and even made his own films.

In the 1890s, Edison began manufacturing the first movie projector, called the "Vitascope."

A scene from the film *The Great Train Robbery*

The Great Train Robbery was the most famous movie that Edison produced. Moviegoers were thrilled. They loved the story about law and order in the Old West.

Thomas Edison created and improved so many gadgets and machines that it would take pages and pages to list them all. In 1931, this great inventor died at the age of 84 at his New Jersey home. As a tribute to him, lights were turned off all across the United States for one minute on the night of his funeral.

In 1927, Thomas Edison took part in a radio broadcast to celebrate the 50th anniversary of his invention of the phonograph.

Glossary

carbon (KAR-buhn) A chemical element found in coal and in all living things

electric current (i-LEK-trik KUR-uhnt) A flow of electricity through a wire

electric car (i-LEK-trik KAR) A car that has an electric motor and that uses energy stored in a rechargeable battery instead of using gasoline

filament (FIL-uh-muhnt) A fine wire or thread that glows and produces light

incandescent (in-kan-DESS-uhnt) Glowing as a result of being heated

investor (in-VEST-uhr) A person who gives money to a project in the belief that he or she will get money back in the future

laboratory (LAB-ruh-tor-ee) A room or building containing special equipment for people to use in scientific experiments

manufacturer (man-yoo-FAK-chur-uhr) A business that makes things in large amounts, often with the use of machinery

patent (PAT-uhnt) A legal document giving an inventor the sole right to manufacture or sell an invention

phonograph (FOH-nuh-graf) A machine that picks up and reproduces sounds that have been recorded in the grooves cut into a record

rechargeable storage battery (ree-CHAR-jih-buhl STOR-ij BAT-uh-ree) A battery that uses electricity to restore its energy when it is used up

stocks (STOKS) Shares of ownership in a company

telegraph (TEL-uh-graf) A system for sending messages over long distances; it uses a code of electrical signals sent by wire or radio

vacuum (VAK-yoom) A sealed space from which all air has been emptied

Index